Systems of Government

DICTATORSHIP

Sean Connolly

W
FRANKLIN WATTS
LONDON • SYDNEY

 An Appleseed Editions book

First published in 2013 by Franklin Watts
338 Euston Road, London NW1 3BH

Franklin Watts Australia
Hachette Children's Books
Level 17/207 Kent St, Sydney, NSW 2000

© 2012 Appleseed Editions

Created by Appleseed Editions Ltd,
Well House, Friars Hill, Guestling,
East Sussex TN35 4ET

Designed by Hel James
Edited by Mary-Jane Wilkins
Picture research by Su Alexander

ISBN 978 1 4451 0988 6

Dewey Classification 321.9

A CIP catalogue for this book is available from the British Library.

Picture credits
page 5 Popperfoto/Getty Images; 7 Getty Images; 9 Time & Life Pictures/Getty
Images; 10 & 12 Getty Images; 14 Elen/Shutterstock; 16 Getty Images; 17 Ligak/
Shutterstock; 18 & 20 AFP/Getty Images; 22 Thinkstock; 24 Eugenio Marongiu/
Shutterstock; 26 Gammarapho/Getty images; 28 & 31 Getty Images; 32 Ryan Rodrick
Beiler/Shutterstock; 34 & 36 Gammarapho via Getty Images; 38 Svic/Shutterstock;
40 & 42 AFP/Getty Images; 44 De Visu/Shutterstock

Printed in Malaysia

Franklin Watts is a division of Hachette Children's Books,
an Hachette UK company.
www.hachette.co.uk

Contents

What is a dictatorship?

At break time in a primary school, children stream into the playground. They form little groups – some are skipping, others are playing tag and at the far end of the playground a small crowd of boys jostle to reach the top of a little mound. One of the boys pushes others aside and climbs to the top. From there, it is easy for him to push away anyone else trying to reach him.

'I'm the king of the castle,' the boy at the top cries, 'and you're the dirty rascal,' to anyone who tries to take his place.

Imagine a political system in which the leader is 'king of the castle'. How he got there is unimportant: the main thing is that he is there and everyone else isn't. And once he's there – just like the boy in the school playground – he makes sure that no one else can make it to the top. Rather than pushing others away himself, though, he has loyal followers do his dirty work. They might be members of the army, a special police force or simply people who can hurt or threaten anyone who challenges the leader.

Power, power, power

This system of government is called a **dictatorship**, and the person at the top is a dictator. Dictatorships develop and continue to exist because they rely on power and fear. Adults fear dictators as much as schoolchildren fear the bully standing on the mound in the playground.

On one level, it is easy to see that such a system of government echoes human nature. Strong or forceful people often try to impose their will on others. In some ways, people are no different from wolves or lions – a strong leader will try to lead the pack. Some of the earliest forms of human government, many thousands of years ago, arose from such behaviour. We might think that **monarchies** are full of **rituals** and theatrical customs (such as royal weddings), but the first kings were fierce warriors who forced others to obey them.

TIMELINE... TIMELINE... TIMELINE... TIMELINE... TIMELINE... TIMELINE.

BCE **510** Office of dictator established in Rome to deal with emergencies

This book examines dictators and dictatorships, which still exist in the modern world despite many advances in other aspects of society. How can they exist at a time when news travels around the world in an instant? Surely people have moved on from such brutal forms of government? With mass protests now rocking even the strongest dictatorships, are we witnessing their last gasp, or will future generations still struggle to achieve the most basic human rights in their own countries?

German leader Adolf Hitler stands before cheering crowds in 1934, a year after coming to power.

TIMELINE... TIMELINE... TIMELINE... TIMELINE... TIMELINE... TIMELINE...

356 **Gaius Marcius Rutilus becomes first non-royal Roman dictator**

President for life

Think about the word 'president' for a moment.

You can imagine all sorts of presidents – of clubs, teams, charitable organizations and even of countries. Some presidents might be good at their job; others may be forgotten soon after their term as president ends. None of them, though, will be there for the rest of their lives.

The word 'president' also suggests some sort of choosing or election. Most presidents are elected – aren't they? Even when a presidential election is close or even disputed, the loser usually accepts the outcome as the people's choice. The losing candidate knows – just as all the people in the country know – that the president won't be there forever. He or she can try again, and may be chosen next time.

Now consider the phrase 'president for life'. It seems to go against the very idea of what it is to be a president. Yet many national leaders use that term to describe themselves. Even if they were once elected to the presidency, they are determined not to let anyone else become president. Why? Because they have become dictators, rulers who maintain their position through force rather than popular choice.

What's in a name?

Just what is a dictator? Look at the root of the word – the shorter word, 'dictate'. To dictate is 'to say something aloud so that another can write it down', but the second definition, 'to speak as a superior; to command' is the one that applies to dictators. They tell others what to do, and not just the people who work with or for them: dictators tell the people in their country what to do. They are an extreme example of what people describe as strong leadership – even if they take the idea too far.

To get a fuller understanding of what dictatorships are, it is easier to consider what they are not. One of the most important features of dictatorships is that they are not **democratic**. In other words,

TIMELINE... TIMELINE... TIMELINE... TIMELINE... TIMELINE... TIMELINE.

BCE 49–44   Julius Caesar is Roman dictator until assassinated; opponents fear he is too powerful

their power does not come from the source that underpins the governments of the UK, Australia, the United States, Japan or any country with democratic traditions. Democracies flourish because of free and fair elections.

Dictators and dictatorships are the enemies of people's democratic right to choose a government. They can be **right-wing** or **left-wing**, or sometimes their political viewpoint is less important than simply gaining – and keeping – power. Dictators might take different paths to achieve that power, but once in power they share many qualities.

Seizing power

If voters don't decide to offer such power to a leader, how does someone become a dictator? The short answer is that they seize power. Some dictators are elected fairly, but then take advantage of the power

General Jorge Videla of Argentina (left) and General Augusto Pinochet of Chile exchange greetings in Mendoza, Argentina, close to the border between the two countries in 1978. Military dictatorships held power in both countries at the time.

TIMELINE... TIMELINE... TIMELINE... TIMELINE... TIMELINE... TIMELINE...

CE **1547–1584** Ivan IV (Ivan the Terrible) becomes first Russian tsar; governs with terror

that comes with elected office – especially power over the military and police. They turn on their opponents, arresting them or making their political parties illegal. Step by step, the elected leader gathers more and more power – and few people are able to oppose him.

Other dictators come from the military. Typically, they accuse an elected leader of being weak or lacking the nerve to take tough decisions. These military leaders include Francisco Franco in Spain in the 1930s and Augusto Pinochet in Chile in the 1970s. They used force to topple the elected government. An overthrow of a government is called a *coup d'état* (French for 'a blow or stroke of the **state**').

TOTALITARIANISM

No matter how dictatorships form, they share some characteristics. Most political experts use another word – totalitarianism – to describe the workings of a dictatorship. Again, this word becomes easier to understand if you look at its core word, 'total'. This form of government gives the state total control over every element of public and private life. In other words, the rulers accept no limits on their power.

Totalitarian rulers usually link their aims to a way of thinking called an **ideology**, a system of ideas that sees the world in simple black-and-white terms. **Communist** ideology, for example, holds that private property is bad and that the government should take it from individual people. **Fascist** ideology believes that a country needs to be strong and able to take what it needs from other countries, by force if necessary.

A totalitarian government aims to build support and stay in power by:
• demanding that people support its ideology;
• having just one political party and making it part of the government;
• controlling the armed forces;
• controlling the media and other forms of communication;
• enforcing its rule and spying on its people with a secret police force;
• dictating every aspect of the national economy.

TIMELINE... TIMELINE... TIMELINE... TIMELINE... TIMELINE... TIMELINE.

1653–1658   Oliver Cromwell, who overthrew King Charles I, becomes Lord Protector in England

SPIES AND SECRET POLICE

When films and novels portray people's lives under a dictatorship, they show suspicious-looking men pretending to read newspapers under streetlights while they spy on passers-by. We can assume that they work for – or report to – a powerful force of secret police. What's not spelled out (but we assume) is that the people they spy on might be arrested, taken away and never seen again.

A stern East German policeman stands watch at Checkpoint Charlie, one of the most famous border crossings along the Berlin Wall. The wall, which divided the city of Berlin as well as East and West Germany, was planned by the East German communist leader Walter Ulbricht in 1961.

TIMELINE... TIMELINE... TIMELINE... TIMELINE... TIMELINE... TIMELINE...

1793–1794   Maximilien Robespierre takes power during French Revolution; executes thousands

The power to rule

We often use the words 'left' or 'right' to describe political systems. A government of the left (also called a left-wing system) favours a powerful government role. This means that the government owns many businesses and provides most important services, such as education, medicine and transport (see pages 14–17). A right-wing system goes in the opposite direction, expecting individuals to look after themselves with less government involvement.

TIMELINE... TIMELINE... TIMELINE... TIMELINE... TIMELINE... TIMELINE

1799–1814   Napoleon Bonaparte assumes dictatorial powers in France

President Mobuto Sese Seko of Zaire (which is now known as the Democratic Republic of the Congo) appears before international reporters during an official visit to France in 1978. Mobuto seized control in 1965 and remained in power until 1997. During that time he amassed a huge personal fortune while ruling as a dictator.

Most modern, democratically-run countries have political parties on both the left and the right. If voters think that one of the parties has gone too far, they will choose the other party at the next election – or a party that is in the centre, or middle ground. So it is common to see countries move a little to the left, then to the right, and then back again in successive elections.

Concentration of power

Democratic parties of the right or left have to respond to voters' preferences to stay in power. That means that they can never go too far with their plans. This can change when extreme parties gain ground – which often happens through coups (see below) or **revolution**.

People with extreme right-wing views often portray themselves as the country's only **patriots**. When a government of the left or centre holds power, they complain that the country has become weaker and that it should stand up and promote 'strong values' of loyalty and obedience.

Many right-wing dictators began by being elected to office in democratic elections. The notorious German dictator Adolf Hitler came to power in 1933 when his Nazi party promised an end to the chaos and confusion Germany had faced since it had been defeated in the **First World War**. Within months, Hitler had forced other elected officials to give him more and more power to make laws and govern. From 1934 until his death in 1945, Hitler proved a cruel dictator, provoking the **Second World War** in which tens of millions of people died.

A link between right-wing dictatorships and the military is very common. Many dictators have been military leaders who overthrew elected governments (usually claiming that those governments were weak). This type of violent overthrow is called a *coup d'état* (see page 8) and because such right-wing governments come to power through military involvement, the country's armed forces remain at the heart of power.

TIMELINE... TIMELINE... TIMELINE... TIMELINE... TIMELINE... TIMELINE...

1804–1806   Jean-Jacques Dessalines abandons democracy in Haiti, assuming title of Emperor

Colonial history

Countries such as Nigeria and Pakistan have been ruled by both democratically elected and military governments during the 50 or 60 years they have been independent. Like many countries in Africa and Asia, they were once **colonies** of European powers. Long before those European countries prepared to hand over power in the mid-twentieth century, they had established military schools to train local people to take over from the European armed forces stationed there.

The military establishments remained active, producing some of the best-educated people in those countries. Unfortunately, the Europeans

Pakistan has been under military control for much of the time since it gained independence in 1947. Before that, it was under British colonial rule. These Pakistani trainee soldiers perform drills based on those of the British army.

TIMELINE... TIMELINE... TIMELINE... TIMELINE... TIMELINE... TIMELINE.

1856–1857   American William Walker seizes power in Nicaragua, but is eventually executed

often provided fewer opportunities for local people to train as teachers, lawyers, doctors or other professionals. This legacy made it harder for democratic elections to produce well-trained leaders – and easier for the military in those countries to complain that they were the only people capable of government.

As a result of this colonial history, many military governments claim to be in power temporarily, until the country is ready to hold democratic elections. The government might not consider itself to be a dictatorship, but many such governments have all the trappings of dictatorship – they deny people some basic **civil rights**, operate powerful networks of secret police, and favour one tribe, religious group or region over others in the country.

FULL CIRCLE?

Although the terms left and right suggest violent (and permanent) political divisions, sometimes the extremes at either end of the spectrum come to resemble each other. For someone living in a democratic country such as Britain or the United States in the late 1930s, the political systems of Germany (far right) and the **Soviet Union** (far left) seemed as bad as each other. Secret police snooped on ordinary people in both countries, and the government came to control much of the information that those people received. Some of this blurring exists even today: would outsiders prefer to live in North Korea (a communist dictatorship) or in Fiji (under military rule)?

THE VOTING BOOTH

Time to hand over?

Can you think of circumstances in which it would be a good thing for the military to take power in a country? Maybe during a **civil war**? Possibly after a huge natural disaster such as an earthquake? If you think military power is acceptable for short periods, how do you think the soldiers who take charge can be persuaded to hand back power to civilians?

TIMELINE... TIMELINE... TIMELINE... TIMELINE... TIMELINE... TIMELINE...

1879–1910   Porfirio Diaz gains control Mexico, modernizing at the expense of the poor

Left turn only

The most extreme left-wing governments are called communist. Many of them come to power through revolutions that promised to improve conditions for ordinary people who had suffered under previous governments. According to communist promises, those ordinary people, who make up the majority of most countries, would become the new rulers. It seems like an ideal system: no one need go hungry or lack a job, and because these governments promise fairness and equality, they call themselves democracies.

TIMELINE... TIMELINE... TIMELINE... TIMELINE... TIMELINE... TIMELINE.

1922–1943   Benito Mussolini establishes a strong fascist government in Italy

DICTATORSHIP OF THE PROLETARIAT

Most communist governments do not shy away from using the word dictatorship to describe themselves. A phrase often used is 'dictatorship of the **proletariat**'. The nineteenth-century architects of communism, Karl Marx and Friedrich Engels, often used it to describe a form of government that could replace a **capitalist** system.

Under this form of dictatorship, the proletariat, or working class, would band together to rule in its own interest. That would mean making life harder for factory owners and rich people who, Marx and Engels believed, held all the power under capitalism. So the power in this type of dictatorship would be shared by many people – all of whom would be elected, according to the theory – rather than one leader enforcing his will on those around him.

Actors portraying Vladimir Lenin (left) and Josef Stalin – two of the first Soviet communist leaders – stroll through a park devoted to the history of communism in Moscow.

Unfortunately, most communist systems have failed to live up to this promise. The communist leaders believe that the ordinary people who should be the new rulers are too poorly educated to look after their own affairs and need guidance. And who do they think should provide this guidance? The people who staged the revolution, of course.

The idea behind communism presented by Karl Marx in the nineteenth century, was one of mass involvement. The vast majority of people in any country – factory workers and farmers – would gain control of the government. Marx believed that this would happen naturally. In real life it proved more difficult. Vladimir Lenin, leader of the **Russian Revolution** of 1917, decided that ordinary Russians were not yet ready to look after their affairs in true communist style. Some of them even opposed the idea – out of ignorance, Lenin believed. He proposed a new style of communism (called Marxist-Leninist), in which a small group of educated people looked after the needs of the masses.

So the left-wing ideal of a government representing all the people – and managed by those people – went out of the window. Instead, a small group of people govern and decide what is best for the country. Very often, one of that small group of leaders gains power over the others and becomes, in effect, the sole ruler of the country.

TIMELINE... TIMELINE... TIMELINE... TIMELINE... TIMELINE... TIMELINE...

1927–1975   Chiang Kai-Shek rules by force in China, then in Taiwan after Mao Zedong takes over in China

Cubans celebrate May Day, the main communist holiday, with a photograph of Cuban leader Fidel Castro in 2007.

VOICE OF THE PEOPLE

NO OUTSIDE INFORMATION

Life Funds for North Korean Refugees (LFNKR) is an international organization which helps people who escape from the dictatorship that rules North Korea. These refugees provide one of the few sources of accurate information about life under the brutal dictatorship.

One of them, known as 'Ms Kim', managed to cross the border into China, where she stayed in an LFNKR shelter. Her story is similar to that of other refugees: "Few people in our village ever try to escape from North Korea, because almost no outside information reaches our village, which is far inland. Most of them don't even know that they could get enough food to fill their stomachs here in China. If they knew, I'm sure they would all try to flee to China. Most of the villagers believe that the people in all other countries are living lives like their own. A few people in the village who tried to flee into China were arrested. Unlike villages near the border, the punishments are much more severe in our village, since it is located inland. Hardly anyone ever comes out of the jails alive."

TIMELINE... TIMELINE... TIMELINE... TIMELINE... TIMELINE... TIMELINE.

1928   Josef Stalin becomes leader of the Soviet Union

THE BUNKER MENTALITY

Enver Hoxha was the brutal communist ruler of Albania for 40 years until his death in 1985. He kept the tiny East European country cut off from the outside world, using **propaganda** to tell them that they were constantly under threat of attack. To prove his point, he ordered that nearly a million bunkers – roughly one for each Albanian – should be built along Albania's borders.

Hoxha's imaginary enemies never attacked, but the Albanians paid for his extravagant gesture. The money spent on the **bunkers** could have been used to build half a million flats – enough for everyone to live in comfort. Instead, most Albanians led impoverished lives.

These concrete bunkers are some of thousands built by the dictator Enver Hoxha to protect Albania from invasion. They stand as reminders of the country's harsh communist past.

TIMELINE... TIMELINE... TIMELINE... TIMELINE... TIMELINE... TIMELINE...

1930–1961   Rafael Trujillo become dictator of Dominican Republic, and encourages racist murder

Back by popular demand...

Dictators often justify their brutal policies by saying that the country needs firm government – without their decisive action, they argue, the country would descend into chaos. This leads on to their belief that they have the right to suspend basic civil rights such as free speech and freedom to gather in public.

TIMELINE... TIMELINE... TIMELINE... TIMELINE... TIMELINE... TIMELINE.

1932–1968	Antonio de Salazar rules Portugal as a fascist dictatorship
1933–1945	Adolf Hitler leads Germany as a Nazi dictator
1937–1956	Anastasio Somoza Garcia seizes power in Nicaragua and becomes enormously wealthy

Elections take on a different meaning in such societies. Dictators either abandon the whole idea of democratic elections, arguing that they would lead to disagreements and confusion, or they hold elections that would seem laughable in any democratic country. These elections often have no opposition candidates and the number of votes the government claims have been cast in their favour often exceeds the number of voters in the country (see chart).

Soldiers emerge from voting booths during the 2010 general election in Belarus, a country known for its harsh regime. No one was surprised when President Alexander Lukashenko won his fourth five-year term of office.

EXTREME VOTING RESULTS IN DICTATORSHIPS

1930   Rafael Trujillo is elected president of the Dominican Republic, receiving more votes than there are registered voters.

1953   The government of Mohamed Reza Pahlavi, the Shah of Iran, receives 100% of the vote in an election that registers more votes than there are voters.

1983   Paul Biya, the only candidate, wins 99% of the vote and rules Cameroon for more than three decades.

2002   Saddam Hussein wins 100% of the vote in a **referendum** on keeping him in power in Iraq.

2003   Kim Jong-il is re-elected with 100% of the vote, showing that North Korea resists outside interference.

2006   Alexander Lukashenko, leader of Belarus since 1994, gains 83% of the vote.

2008   Meles Zenawi's Ethiopian People's Revolutionary Democratic Front party wins 99.6% of the vote.

2009   North Korea's government-controlled **news agency** announces another Kim Jong-il victory, as he captures 99.98% of the vote.

2009   Ben Ali is elected president of Tunisia with 98.6% of the vote; a popular uprising forces him to resign less than two years later.

2010   Paul Kagame is re-elected president of Rwanda, securing 93% of the vote.

TIMELINE... TIMELINE... TIMELINE... TIMELINE... TIMELINE... TIMELINE...

1939–1975	Francisco Franco rules Spain as a fascist dictatorship
1944–1980	Josip Broz Tito governs Yugoslavia as a dictatorship with communist influence
1944–1985	Enver Hoxha establishes a strict communist dictatorship in Albanias

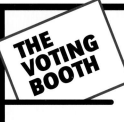

THE VOTING BOOTH

Who are they kidding?

Outside observers of 'election' results in dictatorships are either amused or angry. How can a dictator pretend that he has been fairly elected (or re-elected) when there's no other choice or when he claims to have received every vote in the country? Can making such announcements have any positive effect for the ruler?

TIMELINE... TIMELINE... TIMELINE... TIMELINE... TIMELINE... TIMELINE.

1948–1994   Kim Il-Sung becomes the first leader of communist North Korea and rules for 46 years

1949   Mao Zedong establishes a communist government in China, imprisoning or executing opponents

1953   Stalin dies, and his successors move the Soviet Union away from dictatorship

TARGETING WHITE FARMERS

Robert Mugabe was elected prime minister of Zimbabwe in the country's first elections after it became independent in 1980. Before that, a minority white government had ruled the country then called Rhodesia, which was a former British colony. Mugabe was a popular figure, who had led one of the rebel forces that toppled the Rhodesian government and paved the way for the new, democratic Zimbabwe.

As leader, Mugabe faced opposition from another former rebel, Joshua Nkomo, and his armed forces. Their clash came close to becoming a civil war, and by the time it ended in 1998 it was clear that Mugabe had neglected Zimbabwe's economy. Zimbabwe's fertile soil and good climate should have produced abundant crops, but farmers were struggling to produce enough food for everyone. Mugabe was blamed for this decline and became unpopular.

In 2000, Mugabe began a programme to redistribute land in the country. White farmers who had remained in the country after independence were targeted. Mugabe claimed that his plan – which effectively forced white farmers off their farms – would distribute land more fairly among Zimbabweans. He may have thought that the move would increase his popularity, but the country's economy then collapsed. Many white Zimbabweans were driven out of the country and the people who took over their farms had no experience of large-scale farming. Yet Mugabe continued to tell Zimbabweans that their problems came from outside the country, and not from his policies. Armed police maintained a menacing presence in major towns and cities, ready to round up anyone suspected of opposing the government.

A policeman (right) guards the new occupants of a farm near Harare, the capital of Zimbabwe, in April 2000. Zimbabwean leader Robert Mugabe (whose photograph is on display) had encouraged young black men to take over farms which belonged to the country's white population.

TIMELINE... TIMELINE... TIMELINE... TIMELINE... TIMELINE... TIMELINE...

1953–1979	Mohammad Reza Pahlavi rules as Shah (emperor) of Iran; abolishes rival political parties
1954–1984	Ahmed Sékou Touré imposes dictatorship in the west African state of Guinea
1954–1989	Alfredo Stroessner gains power in Paraguay and establishes a brutal dictatorship

21

The trains run on time

If dictatorships rely on fear and force to stay in power, how can they make people obey them, rather than rising up in rebellion? Surely they would need soldiers posted at every street corner? And wouldn't that level of spending topple a government, even without uprisings and rebellions?

Japan was one of the few nations to repel the military advance of the Mongol empire. Its warriors withstood two invasions in the late thirteenth century – helped by the arrival of a typhoon that sank the Mongol fleet in 1281.

TIMELINE... TIMELINE... TIMELINE... TIMELINE... TIMELINE... TIMELINE.

1957–1971   Francois (Papa Doc) Duvalier declares himself president for life in Haiti and crushes opposition

ANOTHER SIDE TO GENGHIS KHAN?

Today, we are aware of major problems such as global warming, which is linked to the carbon dioxide and other gases that cars and factories send into the Earth's atmosphere. The carbon dioxide acts as a blanket, trapping heat below and causing global temperatures to rise. At the same time, people are cutting down huge areas of forest to make way for cities and housing and to provide more land for farmers.

Now scientists have come up with one positive outcome for the Earth of the actions of Genghis Khan – one of the most cruel and ruthless dictators in history. How could this be? The answer lies in Genghis Khan's conquests. Beginning in 1206 CE, he created a Mongol empire that covered more than a fifth of the world's land. Historians estimate that as his Mongol horsemen swept across Asia and Europe, they killed 40 million people. When so many people died, forests grew once again to cover the huge areas of farmland they had cultivated.

Forests absorb carbon dioxide from the atmosphere. Scientists believe that 700 million tones of carbon were absorbed during the Mongol era (the thirteenth and fourteenth centuries): that is the same amount that all the world's cars pump into the atmosphere every year.

The answer is complicated and involves an understanding of human nature. First of all, dictators can instil fear with fewer armed soldiers than we might imagine. By using secret police, they can create a mood of uncertainty. People living under a dictatorship are likely to stop and wonder: 'Is it safe to be seen with this writer?' or 'Can I trust that woman to read this letter of protest?' or 'What if my son's teacher sees him with that foreign newspaper?' As a result, many people choose to play safe and not risk being arrested by someone dressed in civilian clothes.

Propaganda

Another way to keep people loyal is to convince them that the government is accomplishing things on their behalf. These might be victories in wars of conquest or improvements to the way people live. If dictators use propaganda skilfully, they can persuade people to believe their claims even if they are false. Yulia Tymoshenko, the former prime minister of Ukraine, was jailed in October 2011 because of energy deals she had made with neighbouring Russia while in power. She argued that the new Ukrainian government was really a dictatorship because it was using propaganda to distort the truth.

One successful user of propaganda was Benito Mussolini, who came to power in Italy in 1922 and ruled as a fascist dictator until he died in 1943. Italy has a reputation for being disorganized, yet people came to believe that under Mussolini, 'the trains ran on time'. Punctual trains became a symbol of fascist efficiency, even if modern historians accuse Mussolini of distorting the truth.

The imposing Stazione Centrale (main station) in Milan was built during the government of Benito Mussolini. Its design suggests the power of the Italian people as well as the popular belief that the dictator 'made the trains run on time'.

1962–1968   Ne Win seizes power in Burma in a coup and establishes a brutal dictatorship

VOICE OF THE PEOPLE

HOPE, THEN DISAPPOINTMENT
Robert Mugabe had been one of the main leaders in the movement to help Zimbabwe become independent. So in 1980, he was a popular choice to become prime minister. But then he abolished the position of prime minister in 1987 and has remained president ever since. Much of the early hope Mugabe inspired has evaporated as his government has become more of a dictatorship.

This letter writer to the Zimbabwe Independent *newspaper was a child when Mugabe was first elected: "Though I did not know much about him, I was happy that the country was now free. I looked forward to a better Zimbabwe and a lot of changes that the majority of people would benefit from. In the early 1980s Mugabe became the people's choice and indeed a household name. One would freeze everything and listen attentively to a live broadcast of his speech either on national radio or television. The young, the old, the poor and the rich black people liked him."*

The writer goes on to describe his disappointment that Mugabe has failed to live up to his promises about education, health, jobs and taxes. Instead, according to the writer, Mugabe blames all the country's problems on outsiders and people from the past: "For far too long Mugabe has dwelt in the past. While we need to be conscious of our history and the liberation struggle, we cannot spend 30 years preaching hate language every day and doing so little to address real issues that need urgent attention."

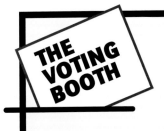

THE VOTING BOOTH

A trade-off
Would you be willing to give up a few basic rights in order to have a stronger country? If a dictator promised to make the streets safe (by ordering soldiers to patrol them, for example), would you support the idea?

TIMELINE... TIMELINE... TIMELINE... TIMELINE... TIMELINE... TIMELINE...

1966–1979   Jean-Bédel Bokassa, dictator of the Central African Republic; declares himself emperor in 1976

The flow of power

At the heart of most dictatorships is an overriding concern with power – how to achieve it, how to retain it and how to pass it on to a chosen successor. In each of these areas, dictatorships operate along different lines from democracies and other representative forms of government.

Haitian dictator Jean-Claude 'Baby Doc' Duvalier stands solemnly at an official gathering in April 1978. He had taken over from his father, 'Papa Doc' Duvalier, seven years earlier and governed with the same rule of terror – as the gun in his right hand shows.

TIMELINE... TIMELINE... TIMELINE... TIMELINE... TIMELINE... TIMELINE.

1967–1997   Suharto rules Indonesia as a military dictatorship

KILLING RUNS IN THE FAMILY

Francois Duvalier was a doctor who began his career combating deadly diseases in his native country, Haiti. His nickname was Papa Doc. Duvalier was elected president of Haiti in 1957, but soon abandoned any attempt to support democracy in his country. In 1964, he declared himself president for life and ruled until his death in 1971. Papa Doc's Haiti became a place of fear, where people disappeared and Duvalier's wishes were carried out by a frightening police force known as the Tontons Macoutes (the local term for bogeymen).

When Papa Doc died in 1971, his son Jean-Claude (nicknamed Baby Doc) took over. Baby Doc also ruled as a dictator and was eventually driven from Haiti in 1986. Baby Doc returned to Haiti in January 2011, promising to help the country that had recently been hit by a terrible earthquake and a devastating hurricane. Instead, he was arrested and accused of corruption during his years in power.

Many in Haiti were eager to see Baby Doc brought to justice. But some, like the democracy supporter Jean-Claude Bajeux, believe the story is a little more complicated: "He inherited a system of government that was based on killing people. I think that was the tragedy of this guy. He was not aware of the monstrosity of what he was doing every day. To him, killing people and torturing people was normal life."

Democratic leaders are chosen by the voters in their country. They retain power – and may be re-elected – if they fulfil most of their promises and steer the country wisely. Who the next leader will be is also up to the voters, although an outgoing leader can try to persuade voters to choose a particular candidate.

Dictators usually use – or threaten to use – force to become national leaders. Once in power, they use similar methods to encourage obedience and loyalty; opposing political views are stifled and opposition leaders arrested or even killed. They have no reservations about using violence and threats, so dictators feel that the idea of who will succeed them is just another decision they should take and strictly enforce.

TIMELINE... TIMELINE... TIMELINE... TIMELINE... TIMELINE... TIMELINE...

1967–2005   Gnassingbé Eyadéma gains power in Togo, banning, torturing or killing opposition

Preparing the way

The route to leadership for a dictator is similar to that taken by kings long ago – defeating rivals with force and power. So it is not surprising that dictators often choose their own children to take over power when they are gone, just as **hereditary** rulers do.

Oliver Cromwell led the armed forces of England's Parliament against King Charles I during a brutal civil war. After the king's forces were defeated (and Charles beheaded in 1649), Parliament gave Cromwell more powers. By 1653 he had the title of Lord Protector, which in some ways gave him more power than a king. Cromwell had to choose a successor, so when he died in 1658 his son Richard became Lord Protector.

Parent-to-child succession remains common in many dictatorships to this day. Papa Doc Duvalier, Haiti's powerful leader, was succeeded by his son, Baby Doc when he died in 1971 (see Voice of the people). When North Korean dictator Kim Il-Sung died in 1994, his son Kim Jong-il took over. The North Korean **constitution** considered Kim Il-Sung to be the country's eternal leader.

Richard Cromwell became Lord Protector (a virtual dictator) of Britain after his father, Oliver Cromwell, died in 1658. Richard, however, had few of his father's political skills and was forced from his position after less than a year.

Opposing voices

Dictators are always concerned about numbers – and so they should be as they are vastly outnumbered by the people they rule. Democratically-elected leaders know that many of their country's citizens voted for them, and that many of the others (who voted against them) are prepared to give them a chance to succeed. That second group can vote for a rival – or opposition – political party in the next election.

A dictator, on the other hand, must consider all the country's citizens as potential enemies. After all, none of them chose the dictator and there is usually no legal way of removing a dictator from power, if there are no free elections. But when all the power is controlled by one person or small group, how can the majority of people voice their disapproval?

Fear and courage
Dictators hope that people will remain under their control through a combination of fear and ignorance. They often stage military parades to mark special occasions. According to the government, these displays

THE VOTING BOOTH

Playing politics
Many political leaders in democracies can become impatient with opposition parties, accusing them of 'playing politics' when they dwell on issues that embarrass the government. The same governments might go on to say that constantly attacking an elected government's reputation is bad for the country – and in times of war, even helpful to the enemy. Do you think that there should be limits to how far opposition leaders should go in their criticism, or do you think that might be the first step towards dictatorship?

TIMELINE... TIMELINE... TIMELINE... TIMELINE... TIMELINE... TIMELINE...

1968–1991	Moussa Trouré turns the African nation of Mali into a harsh **police state**

New forms of communication

Modern technology has made it easier for people to exchange ideas – and to criticize governments and even plan revolts – in many dictatorships. It is easier to censor or close down newspapers and magazines because they are physical products that can be collected and destroyed. Television and radio offer a better chance of getting messages across, but even that information must be broadcast from a station. Police in dictatorships usually close down independent television and radio stations and broadcast their own messages.

Mobile phones and the Internet are a different matter. These new generation forms of communication are instant and link individuals with each other; they have no central point that can be shut down. Recent protests in Iran, Tunisia, Bahrain, Libya and Egypt have all developed through people texting each other or passing on information via social network websites.

Nearly 400 million people can now access the Internet in China – about ten times more than in 2000. Although the Chinese government does its best to block websites that it views as threatening, computer experts often manage to get past these controls. The news and information that people exchange is often unaffected by the government, and very different from the official news broadcast through the government media.

Yasheng Huang, a Chinese communications expert now teaching in the US, sums up the position in his home country: "China may not have free speech, but it has freer speech, because the Internet has provided a platform for Chinese citizens to communicate with each other."

reassure people that the government can defend them against enemies, but the array of troops and weapons serves to warn citizens of how harshly the government can deal with opposition.

When secret police lurk, ready to invite suspected political opponents into police stations for questioning, the atmosphere of fear worsens. People need enormous courage to raise their voices in protest. But these brave opponents of dictatorship know that once their message is heard – if they can communicate it to others in their country – then others may join in and the days of dictatorship could be numbered.

TIMELINE... TIMELINE... TIMELINE... TIMELINE... TIMELINE... TIMELINE.

1969   Colonel Muammar Gaddafi seizes power in Libya and crushes opposition

Anti-government protesters charge their mobile phones for free outside an electronics shop in Cairo in February 2011. Many people credit mobile phones and the Internet with helping the Egyptians to topple the harsh government of Hosni Mubarak.

VOICE OF THE PEOPLE

FOLLOWING THE YOUNG

Mohamed El Baradei, a Nobel prize-winning scientist and diplomat, has long called for democratic change in his native Egypt. Many see him as a popular choice to replace Hosni Mubarak, who ruled Egypt harshly for more than 30 years. El Baradei returned to Egypt in January 2011 to find the country in the midst of fierce anti-Mubarak protests. It was not longstanding critics of Mubarak who had sparked the protests, but Egypt's young people. As El Baradei noted: "It was the young people who took the initiative and set the date [for the uprising] and decided to go. Frankly, I didn't think the people were ready... [but what the youth have done] will give them the self-confidence they needed."

TIMELINE... TIMELINE... TIMELINE... TIMELINE... TIMELINE... TIMELINE...

1970–2000   Hafez al-Hassad gains power after a coup in Jordan, ruling with no opposition

The outside world

It is hard for outsiders to watch as people in another country suffer at the hands of a brutal dictator. Most people, at one time or another, say to themselves, "Surely there must be something we can do to stop this." This response is natural, but in the real world of international politics it is hard to decide what can be done.

Some obvious questions arise, such as, "If we send in troops to topple that government, then what about similar ones around the world?" People may also worry that a dictator may take outside involvement as evidence that opposition is unpatriotic and simply a foreign effort to take over the country. Libya's Colonel Gaddafi used that argument in March 2011, when British soldiers were arrested on their way to meet opposition leaders.

A Palestinian woman holds a cartoon of Libyan dictator Colonel Muammar Gaddafi, during a protest in East Jerusalem in February 2011. Widespread public protests during the 'Arab spring' of 2011 toppled dictatorships across the Middle East and North Africa.

NOBEL PEACE PRIZE

Receiving a **Nobel Peace Prize** is an exceptional honour for an individual, but also for their country. The committee that decides each year's winner can sometimes make political statements in their choices – especially if the winner is someone who has worked hard to dismantle a dictatorship in his or her country. Dictators must take notice, because even they must realize how the world might react if they mistreated a citizen of their country who has been honoured in this way.

Below are some Nobel Peace Prize winners whose award made a political statement:
1960: Albert Lutuli, leader of the African National Congress, which worked to overthrow South Africa's **apartheid** government.
1975: Andrei Sakharov, for promoting **disarmament** and promoting human rights, especially in his own country, the Soviet Union.
1980: Adolfo Perez Esquivel, of Argentina, for founding non-violent human rights organizations to work against the Argentine military dictatorship.
1983: Poland's Lech Walesa, for promoting human rights in his country and in other communist regimes.
1991: Aung San Suu Kyi, for opposing the military dictatorship in her native Burma.
2010: Liu Xiabo, for promoting human rights within the communist regime of China.

TIMELINE... TIMELINE... TIMELINE... TIMELINE... TIMELINE... TIMELINE...

1971–1986   Jean-Claude (Baby Doc) Duvalier succeeds his father in Haiti; continues harsh regime

Aung San Suu Kyi, leader of Burma's main political party, works at home in 1996. Her party received the most votes in a 1990 general election, but Burma's military rulers refused to accept the result. Everything changed in 2011 when a quasi-civilian government took over. Aung San Suu Kyi is now an elected member of parliament.

VOICE OF THE PEOPLE

SIMPLE DEMANDS

The Libyan uprising of 2011 was typical of several that swept across the Arab world at around the same time. World leaders watched as history was made and were eager to show their support for those pressing for change in oppressive regimes. US president Barack Obama was struck by a statement made by one of the Libyan protesters, and quoted it: "As one Libyan said, 'We just want to be able to live like human beings'... We just want to be able to live like human beings. It is the most basic of aspirations that is driving this change. Throughout this time of transition, the United States will continue to stand up for freedom, stand up for justice, and stand up for the dignity of all people."

TIMELINE... TIMELINE... TIMELINE... TIMELINE... TIMELINE... TIMELINE

| 1973–1990 | General Augusto Pinochet overthrows Chile's elected government; establishes a harsh regime |

Patient watching

The **League of Nations**, which was set up after the First World War, and the **United Nations**, which replaced it after the Second World War, have tried to promote world peace. Both these organizations could have acted as international policemen, moving into a country that failed to live up to agreed standards of behaviour towards its own people. But the UN's rules only allow its peacekeeping forces to go into a region if both sides in the dispute agree to it. Dictators rarely invite outside peacekeepers to check up on them. Instead, the UN uses measures such as imposing **sanctions** to put pressure on dictatorships to change.

Outside leaders sometimes move into countries without UN approval. For example, in 1991 the UN approved an attack on Iraq; troops from 34 countries took part in the Gulf War, driving Iraqi troops from Kuwait. Iraq's dictator Saddam Hussein suffered a major defeat just weeks later.

Twelve years on, the US and the UK led another attack on Iraq – while the UN was still deciding on the best way to deal with Saddam Hussein. Like the first Gulf War, the invasion succeeded, but the cost in lives was much higher. Troops from the invading countries stayed in Iraq long after Saddam Hussein was defeated, arrested and executed. Iraq at times seemed about to explode in a civil war. US president George W. Bush and British prime minister Tony Blair argued that they had freed the Iraqi people by removing a dictator. Many others – including people in the US and UK – wondered whether the invasion had been justified.

Crossing a line

At what point do images of people being arrested (or tortured or executed) demand an international response? 'Stay out of our affairs' and 'mind your own business' are typical responses from governments accused of being harsh dictatorships. Should the outside world ignore those calls and force changes anyway? And if it does, can it decide not to move into other trouble spots in the future? Who do you think should make such choices?

TIMELINE... TIMELINE... TIMELINE... TIMELINE... TIMELINE... TIMELINE...

1974–1991   Mengitsu Haile rules Ethiopia as a communist dictatorship

Fallen idols

How do dictatorships end – and what happens to dictators once their regime is dismantled?

Dictators overthrown in wartime often meet the harshest ends. Benito Mussolini was shot by his Italian opponents in the last weeks of the Second World War. His body was hung upside down in Milan and passers-by jeered and threw stones at it. Mussolini's ally Adolf Hitler took his own life days later as Germany faced defeat.

DICTATOR ON TRIAL

Jean-Bédel Bokassa led an army coup which seized power in the Central African Republic (CAR) in 1965. Seven years later he declared himself president for life and in 1976 he changed the name of the country to the Central African Empire. In 1977, he had himself crowned emperor in a lavish ceremony that cost $20 million – a huge expense for one of the world's poorest countries.

Bokassa's behaviour became even more extreme, he spent recklessly and committed astonishing acts of cruelty. People who protested about the lack of food were shot, and in April 1979 Bokassa's forces attacked a group of schoolchildren who had been protesting about having to wear heavy uniforms with Bokassa's picture on them. About 100 children died, and witnesses say that Bokassa himself took part in the beatings.

That incident led to a military coup (supported by French troops) which overthrew Bokassa, who fled the country. Bokassa lived for several years in Ivory Coast and then was allowed to move to France. In 1986 he returned to the Central African Republic and was immediately arrested. Bokassa was charged with 14 different offences, including murder and cannibalism. He was found guilty of all charges (except cannibalism) in 1987 and sentenced to death. The following year, his sentence was changed to life imprisonment, then reduced to a 20 year sentence in 1989. Bokassa was freed in 1993 and remained in the country until his death in 1996.

Cheering Iraqis watch as US soldiers topple a statue of the dictator Saddam Hussein in April 2003. Saddam's brutal regime led his country into disastrous wars and killed thousands of those who opposed it within Iraq itself.

Most dictators are judged by courts in their own countries or in international courts. Slobodan Milosevic, the former dictator of Serbia, died in 2006 while he was being tried for crimes against humanity by a United Nations court. Manuel Noriega, who ruled as a dictator in Panama, was captured during a US invasion in 1989. He has since served long prison sentences in the United States and France for drug offences. Other dictators face justice in their own country (see above).

TIMELINE... TIMELINE... TIMELINE... TIMELINE... TIMELINE... TIMELINE...

| 1976 | Mao Zedong dies | 1977–2004 | Albert René seizes power in the Seychelles |

The tomb of Vladimir Lenin stands outside the walls of the Kremlin, the heart of government in Moscow. It was once the heart of the communist dictatorship, but now the tomb is mainly a tourist attraction.

THE VOTING BOOTH

Fallen leaders

One of the most memorable photographs of 2003 showed joyful Iraqis pulling down a huge statue of Saddam Hussein, the dictator who had ruled them for 24 years. The smashing of the statue symbolized the end of his rule and – the world hoped – the end of dictatorship in Iraq.

A very different story emerged in Moscow. In 1991, Russia got rid of a communist government and adopted a more democratic system. But in the heart of Moscow is a building which still holds the preserved body of Vladimir Lenin, the leader of the revolution that set up the communist system in 1917. From the time of Lenin's death in 1924 until the fall of the Soviet Union in 1991, thousands of people paid their respects every day to the founder of the Soviet state.

Lenin's tomb remains open to the public, and people still file patiently past his body. What should the Russian government do? Should they simply bury the body of the man who many claim paved the way for communist dictatorship? Or should they simply treat the body as a tourist attraction, like the Tower of London or the Colosseum in Rome, both of which are relics of a cruel past?

TIMELINE... TIMELINE... TIMELINE... TIMELINE... TIMELINE... TIMELINE.

1978–1988   Muhammad Zia-ul-Haq rules Pakistan as dictator after seizing power in a coup

VOICE OF THE PEOPLE

A MISSING FAMILY

Svetlana Sbitneva lived in a Siberian village and was 16 when Josef Stalin, the Soviet dictator, died on 5 March 1953. Like other children who had grown up during Stalin's reign, Svetlana had believed that Stalin was another father to her. She returned from school, where they had staged a memorial service, wearing black ribbons in her hair: "We were all crying – we thought it was the end of the world."

Once home, Svetlana climbed up to the roof, where she liked to be alone. But on that day she met her grandmother: "She was sitting there crying and crossing herself in a way I had never seen before. She saw that I had been crying and said: 'Don't worry, dear. I am crying from happiness. Because he killed my family: my sons, my brothers, my husband, my father. Stalin killed them all – leaving only me and your mother.' That was the first time I heard any of this, and then the two of us sat down and cried together, one from joy, one from grief."

LONG MAY HE REIGN...

Many people spend their childhood and much of their adult life under the rule of a single dictator in their country. They cannot picture life in their country without that leader. Imagine living in the countries ruled by the people in this list – the ten longest-reigning political leaders in recent history.

Fidel Castro	Cuba	1959–2008
Chiang Kai-shek	Republic of China	1928–1975
Kim Il-Sung	North Korea	1948–1994
Omar Bongo	Gabon	1967–2009
Muammar al-Gaddafi	Libya	1969–2011
Enver Hoxha	Albania	1944–1985
Francisco Franco	Spain	1936–1975
Gnassingbé Eyadéma	Togo	1967–2005
Josip Broz Tito	Yugoslavia	1943–1980
Antonio de Oliveira Salazar	Portugal	1932–1968

TIMELINE... TIMELINE... TIMELINE... TIMELINE... TIMELINE... TIMELINE...

1979–2003	Saddam Hussein gains control of Iraq and rules as a brutal dictator

Dictatorship and the media

Francis Bacon, the seventeenth-century English scientist, stated that knowledge is power, and variations of this phrase appear in earlier Persian poetry and even the Bible. The meaning is obvious: people gain power (in every sense) by better understanding what is going on around them.

Dictators understand this all too well. They know that if the people they rule learn enough about the wider world – especially

TOTAL CONTROL

Hundreds of thousands of Egyptians protested against President Hosni Mubarak in early 2011, accusing him of becoming a dictator during his 30 years of power. Mubarak responded by cutting off the Internet within Egypt, banning the Arab news agency Al Jazeera and by adopting other measures to control the media.

Such responses to widespread protest are common in countries that fall short of democratic ideals. Usually, though, the government reconnects the country with the flow of information – if only to prove that it is not a dictatorship. In other countries strict control is a way of life. A dictatorship is not embarrassed to muzzle the media and may even accuse the outside world of telling lies. Without a free press, a dictator believes he can do anything he likes.

Travellers read the newspaper in a North Korean railway station beneath a huge painting showing an idealized view of the country. The government is the only source of information in North Korea, so these readers have no other way of hearing news about their own country or about the outside world.

about the rights and opportunities that they are denied – they will become more powerful. That power would almost certainly be used to try to remove the dictator and this is why dictatorships of all types do their best to stifle the flow of information to their people.

THE VOTING BOOTH

Communication clamp-down
Imagine you are a political leader who is being called a dictator by protesting crowds, just as Egyptian president Hosni Mubarak was in early 2011. You have the power to control or even outlaw certain types of communication. Which type of communication would you find the most threatening? How would you deal with them?

TIMELINE... TIMELINE... TIMELINE... TIMELINE... TIMELINE... TIMELINE...

1980   Robert Mugabe elected in Zimbabwe, crushes opposition and remains in power

Some of those efforts might seem comical to outsiders (see panel, right), but many people living under dictatorships know of no other source of information. The newspapers, television and radio – traditional media – are all controlled by the government. New media (mobile phones and computer-related sources of information such as **blogs**, e-mails and social networking) may be out of reach of most people or blocked by the government.

Mobile uprisings

China has often clamped down on the flow of information entering and leaving its borders. Like other countries threatened by democratic protests, it has a long history of censoring information on television and radio, as well as on the printed page. In the twenty-first century it has taken steps to control people's access to the Internet, blocking content on websites to

try to dictate what Chinese people can see and hear on their computer screens. It can also monitor Internet use, meaning that the government can tell who is viewing 'anti-government' information. Many of these people then hear the knock of the secret police at their door.

In 2011 a wave of popular protests threatened, and in some cases overthrew, unpopular dictatorships across the Arab world, in Tunisia, then Egypt, then Bahrain and Yemen, and then in Libya. Each of those countries responded by controlling the number of foreign reporters within their borders. But information still escaped, much of it transmitted by civilians using mobile phones or hand-held Internet devices. In this case of dictatorship versus the media, the media – and the people – won.

North Korean leader Kim Jong-il (with sunglasses) visits a government-controlled farm in 2010. The North Korean media claimed that the dictator's 'casual' look inspired other world leaders follow his fashion example.

THE BEST GOLFER IN THE WORLD

Kim Jong-Il was the supreme leader of North Korea from 1994-2011, running a dictatorship that kept the outside world – and its own people – in the dark about how it operated. Over the years, North Korea's government-controlled media made some unusual claims about their leader. Here are some of the 'facts' they presented to North Koreans and the wider world.

Kim Jong-Il:

• was the best golfer in the world. The first time he played golf, he scored a world-record 34 – better than any professional golfer has ever scored. He also scored 11 holes-in-one along the way.

• invented the hamburger in 2004. He came up with the idea of the *gogigyeopbbang* (double bread with meat) as a reward for hard-working university students and their teachers.

• gave birth to a star. Not a film star – a real star. According to the government, Kim was born in a cabin on Korea's holiest mountain. At the moment of his birth, a bright star began to shine in the sky; on the ground, winter turned to spring and rainbows appeared.

TIMELINE... TIMELINE... TIMELINE... TIMELINE... TIMELINE... TIMELINE...

1987–2011   Zine El Abidine Ben Ali agrees to democracy in Tunisia but damages the opposition

Looking ahead

Some people are drawn to power, and they may be willing to ignore other people's feelings (and human rights) to achieve their aims. A local bully might force other children to give him their sweets. A general might recruit a band of supporters to overthrow an elected government. Human history is full of stories of dictators who trample on the lives of others.

The citizens of the world must be constantly on the lookout for cases in which dictators find the way to seize power. People need to use the experience gained by others who have confronted dictatorships to preserve human rights in the future.

TIMELINE... TIMELINE... TIMELINE... TIMELINE... TIMELINE... TIMELINE.

1999– Hugo Chavez elected president of Venezuela but is accused of working against democracy

VOICE
OF THE
PEOPLE

GETTING PAST THE FEAR

Gabriela Mitidieri was born in 1984, a year after Argentina returned to elected government after years of brutal military dictatorship. Like many young people in countries that left dictators behind, she knows that basic human freedoms cannot be taken for granted: "I am the daughter of democracy. That means I have a special responsibility."

Gaby has more at stake than many other young people in Argentina. Her father, Sergio, had been kidnapped, tortured and imprisoned without trial during what became known as the Dirty War. He survived that period, but tried to forget about it. He even told Gaby that scars on his back and neck were sports injuries.

"When I first found out about what happened to my father," Gaby says, "I kept asking myself, 'Why did he live? Why did they let him survive?' Then I read 1984 [a book about brutal dictatorships by the English writer George Orwell], and I realized that he and the others survived to keep the fear alive, and to remind the entire population of the fear. My father is living proof of that."

The past that won't go away: hundreds of supporters of Russia's Communist Party march through Moscow on May Day 2010, calling for a return of the old political system.

A constant battle

Dictators and dictatorships thrive on fear; they fear openness and truth, whether at home or abroad. Some of the first targets of would-be dictators are connected to the free flow of information. At one time, dictators could plunge a country into ignorance by stopping the printing of books and newspapers. When communications advanced, people could sidestep these measures by listening to radio reports, but even radio and television broadcasts can be cut off.

Modern protests against dictatorship – in Burma, Iran and Egypt, for example – have come to rely on mobile phones plus social networking Internet sites such as Facebook and Twitter. It's possible that powerful governments might find ways of stifling even these channels of information, but people will always try to get the message of freedom and democracy across, and they will continue to fight fear.

TIMELINE... TIMELINE... TIMELINE... TIMELINE... TIMELINE... TIMELINE...

2011	Popular uprisings in Libya drive Colonel Gaddafi from power

Glossary

apartheid   A system of government in South Africa from 1948 to 1993 in which only white people had full political rights.

blog   A web page that acts as a discussion focus, so people can respond to comments.

bunker   A shelter used for defence in wartime.

capitalism   A system of government that encourages people to own property and businesses.

civil rights   Basic rights, ensured by a government, which allow people to live in safety and without fear.

civil war   A war between two or more groups trying to gain control of a country.

colony   A country or region controlled by a foreign country.

communism   A system of government that outlaws private ownership of businesses and most property and in which the state controls people's lives and freedoms.

constitution   A document outlining how an organization (or country) is to be governed.

coup d'état   The violent overthrow of a government by a small group of people.

democratic   Describing a type of government that gives people the chance to vote for their leaders – and to remove unpopular leaders.

dictatorship   A form of government in which an individual or small group holds absolute power.

disarmament   The voluntary giving up of weapons.

fascism   A type of government that values the nation more than the individual and gives power to a dictator or small group of leaders while trying to crush opposition.

First World War   The war fought mainly in Europe between 1914 and 1918.

free press   The legal right of newspapers, television, radio and other communicators to report without government control.

hereditary   Passing power from parent to child, or another relative, when a leader dies.

ideology   A strict set of beliefs that govern how people behave.

League of Nations   An international peace-keeping organization that existed from 1919 to 1947.

left-wing   Supporting social change to create a fairer society.

monarchy   A system of government in which an individual (the monarch) holds real or symbolic power as head of a nation.

news agency   A company that reports current events and sells information to newspapers, television and radio stations.

Nobel Peace Prize   An annual prize awarded to an individual or an organization that promotes international peace.

patriot   A person who loves his or her country and is prepared to defend it.

police state   A society in which the government strictly controls people's lives and enforces laws with a strong (and often brutal) police force.

proletariat   The people who work in the lowest-paid jobs, especially in factories.

propaganda   The spreading of news, rumour and sometimes lies to gain political advantage or to hurt the reputation of the opposition.

referendum   A special vote, usually on a single issue, that all voters can decide.

refugee   Someone who flees a country to escape violence or harsh treatment.

revolution   A sudden political change in which an existing government is overthrown by its people.

right-wing   Opposed to social change or attempts to upset traditions.

ritual   A set of actions performed because they symbolize wider beliefs.

Russian Revolution   A revolution that overthrew the Russian monarchy in 1917 and established a communist government in its place.

sanction   The international punishment of a country's government, for example, by refusing to trade with some businesses in that country.

Second World War   The war which began in Europe but spread around the world between 1939 and 1945.

Soviet Union   A communist country, including Russia and 14 other states, that lasted from 1917 to 1991.

state   The government and official institutions of a country.

trade union   A group of people who do the same type of work but work for several employers, who act as a group to negotiate better pay and conditions.

United Nations   An international organization of 162 countries which aims to promote world peace and development.

Books

Dictatorship (Political and Economic Systems) R. Tames (Heinemann Educational, 2007)
Germany 1918-45 (Longman History Project) J. Brooman (Longman, 2001)
Re-discovering the Twentieth Century World: A World Study after 1900 C. Shephard and
  K. Shephard (Hodder Education, 2001)

Websites

Life Funds for North Korean Refugees
www.northkoreanrefugees.com

UNICEF Voices of Youth
www.voicesofyouth.org/en/sections/

United Nations Cyberschoolbus
cyberschoolbus.un.org/

Index